TOMBO

TOMBO

THE BIOGRAPHY OF THOMAS ANTHONY DIFILLIPPO

FRANK DELLAPENNA

CONTENTS

INTRODUCTION

Tombo is his name. It is unusual and, most importantly, unforgettable to anyone who meets him. His real name is Thomas Anthony Di Fillippo, named after his father, a time-honored tradition in families. There are millions named Thomas, who later became Tom or Tommy, but for some reason, Thomas Di Fillippo became Tombo, a unique separation from his father and everyone else.

Why is that important? In most cases, a nickname is not that important, but for Tombo, it defined the unique person he is and what he would become. He was now part of a very small group of people who were known only by their first name. Oprah, Tiger, Barrack, Elvis, Sting, and Tombo. He is in good company for sure, and while he is not as famous as the rest, maybe to those who know him, he is.

His life and his work would change the lives of everyone he knew and even those he never met. This is the story of his life, his legacy, and the reason he was born.

CHAPTER ONE

THE EARLY YEARS...

Tombo was an only child, born in 1947. That was unusual for most families in that era, but to his parents, Thomas Di Fillippo and Lucy Rubino Di Fillippo, Tombo was perhaps all they needed or wanted, or perhaps there was another reason why they never had any other children? For the purpose of this book, it is not necessary or important to know why no other siblings were born. Those are personal to the parents and need to be respected. What is important is that Tombo was born, and he was their pride and joy.

His grandfather, Thomas Di Fillippo, was a dairy farmer who married Claudia Zappacosta, an Italian immigrant from the Abruzzi region of Italy. They arrived separately during the time of the great migration of Italians to America. The marriage was arranged by the families. Once Thomas settled in America, his future wife would arrive for them to marry. However, the marriage was arranged for Claudia's older sister, who refused to leave Italy. So, Claudia arrived as a young woman in her teens, married Thomas, a man much older, and they began their lives together. During this time in history, Italy lost almost one-third of the population who migrated to the United States. Why did so many leave Italy? It is a fair question to ask.

To learn the exact details of this migration period, one might read a book called "La Storia." This fascinating book outlines the political and economic conditions of Italy at that time. The short version of history is that the politicians that controlled Italy at that time benefited people from their region. The money was used to build schools and support businesses in the regions of Italy from Rome and north of Rome, where all of the politicians had particular personal and financial interests.

Those regions south of Rome and Sicily were largely considered an annoyance filled with peasants with problems that the government chose to ignore. The result was that people south of Rome were starving, and their children had no schools to attend. These families south of Rome became frustrated, rightly so, which turned into anger, which turned into a plan to take matters into their own hands to educate their children and try to find a better life. If it meant leaving Italy for opportunities in America, it became a simple choice.

Thus, the great migration to the U.S. began. So, they left by the thousands, and those that established themselves in the U.S. brought other families over and found work for them in mines, making roads, working for the railroad, and building subways. Yes, it was hard work, but it was work and a means to a better life for them and their families.

It was during this tumultuous time in Italy that Thomas Di Fillippo arrived in the United States. It is not clear how he arrived, how he was permitted to enter the U.S., or how he acquired a farm in Devault, PA. But it is safe to assume that someone, most likely from his region of Italy, helped secure passage to the U.S., got through customs, and delivered him to Devault, PA, where eventually he acquired ownership of a dairy farm. Yet the courage to leave one's country, not knowing what may lie ahead, is a testament to his courage and resolve.

Together, Thomas and Claudia raised their children on the farm; Anthony, Thomas, Daniel, Frank, John, Louis, Mary, and Lillian. The farmhouse was filled with children who all worked on the farm in Devault, Pennsylvania, a small village about an hour west of Philadelphia.

Dairy farmers are required to milk cows twice a day, early in the morning, and late afternoon, so there was always plenty of work to do; cows to milk, fields to cultivate, stalls to clean, chickens to feed, a vegetable garden to tend, repairing fences and equipment to maintain. Twelve-hour days were the norm.

During this era, children were not carefree, playing with each other during the day, exploring their surroundings, or wallowing away the afternoon reading. They all seemed to realize instinctively that they were vital to the success of the farm and took their responsibilities seriously. Their lives had a purpose from the time they were born, and they would retain this work ethic in their lives and instill that work ethic with their children once they had families of their own.

As the children got older, they all married and raised their families the two girls, Mary and Lillian, married two brothers from the Alleva family, so one by one, they moved out of the family farmhouse and acquired residences of their own that were all nearby, so they could still help out on the farm when and if needed.

When Tombo was born in 1947, his mother and father were still living in the family farmhouse. Tombo was able to spend time with his grandparents every day during those early years. Eventually, another house was built on the farm, where Tombo's mother and father would remain for the rest of their lives.

It was a modest house that had one room in the front that became the Devault Post Office, and Lucy Di Fillippo became the Postmaster. Everyone in Devault came to the post office for their mail and to exchange news of their families, hardships, upcoming weddings, births, and of course, gossip.

As a result, his mother knew everyone and everything that was going on in the community. The evening meals were filled with daily stories of the people who visited the post office to pick up their mail and what was going on in their lives.

Both his father and mother were very compassionate individuals. They rejoiced to hear of new births, engagements, weddings, and people branching out into other professions. Likewise, those that were sick, hurt, and unable to work or experienced a death in the family were of particular concern to them both. Tom and Lucy made a special effort to comfort those in need and to share their pain. Tom Di Fillippo became the godfather of the community. Not the powerful mob boss engaged in illegal activities, but a true godfather, that looked out for the welfare of everyone and tried to help when he could.

At some point, Tombo's father found a need to create a slaughterhouse to provide beef to the community. Cattle were butchered each week, meat was provided, and people bought it to feed their families. Word spread, and the demand for beef increased. It wasn't long before Thomas Di Fillippo discovered that there was more demand for beef than for milk. Slowly but surely, he watched and listened and decided that his role was to provide beef to others. So, from a dairy farmer, he transitioned into a major beef producer as his list of clients continued to rise.

Soon others were needed to butcher and prepare the meat for consumption, so workers were hired. The business expanded, the slaughterhouse expanded, and more importantly, it gave people jobs to support their families.

Tombo witnessed this transformation of his father from a dairy farmer to a meat producer to an astute businessman. And while he was still a child, he recognized this accomplishment and was proud of his father and wanted probably more than anything for his father to be proud of him.

Tombo was a normal child with many friends and cousins in the neighborhood. So, it was not unusual to share the success of his father with them. As his friends and cousins listened to him tell of the slaughterhouse , it became something they all wanted to experience for themselves. Tombo got permission from his father to bring in all the kids one day to watch a cow being slaughtered from start to finish.

We watched as the animal was killed, then hoisted up by the back legs, leaving the head close to the floor, while the blood of the animal drained on the floor from the cut juggler vein in the neck. Men dressed in aprons covered with blood went to work: first removing the hide and internal organs, cutting the animal in half, then butchering everything that was left. We were awed, maybe even a bit overwhelmed by what we were experiencing. After all, how many children get to visit a slaughterhouse? We all felt a bit honored that we were permitted to watch how it was done.

We understood that cattle were raised to provide beef so we could live. We all ate beef; it is just that we didn't really understand where it came from until that day. It was enlightening.

And while they butchered often, I don't think any of us ever wanted to visit the slaughterhouse again.

Summers were hot, and there were no ponds around, but one year Tom and Lucy decided to have an inground pool installed on their property. The pool was installed by his brother, Louis, a general contractor. It was wonderful and beautiful, and for some strange reason, all of us were allowed to use it whenever we wanted. It even seemed a bit strange to me back then; after all, why would they want all the children from Devault to use their pool?

But it was too much for us to resist, and we often went to the pool even though we didn't know how to swim. Just the joy of feeling cool water on a hot day was pure heaven. Little by little, we all learned to swim. And we all learned to swim in the Di Fillippo pool.

Years later, I learned that there was a swim club called the East Whiteland Swim Club. It was not far from where we lived. What none of us knew is that every Italian American family from Devault applied for membership to that swim club, and they were all denied.

Of course, Tom Di Fillippo knew this and decided to build his own pool for the Italian American children of the neighborhood. Tom Di Fillippo didn't want these children to experience prejudice. It was years before any of us knew about this; that our nationality prevented us from joining the local swim club. It was too embarrassing for our parents to tell us as children; that we were not like other white people and that some people were never going to accept us since our ancestors came from Italy. It is not something we would have understood at that time. And it is not something we understand now.

Tombo attended Charlestown Elementary School from first to sixth grade. Interestingly enough, all of the other Italian American children in Devault went to St. Patrick's Catholic School. He recalled that his mother was not very religious and therefore saw no reason to enroll her only son in a Catholic school where religion was taught. It was a bold stance to take in a community of mostly Italian-Americans who all sent their children to St. Patrick's Catholic School in Malvern, PA.

Tombo described himself as chubby and a below-average student. Once, when he showed his father his report card that had all C's he was afraid his father would be disappointed and scold him. Instead, his father looked at it and said, "It's OK; we're just farmers."

Perhaps not an "A" student, but not everyone has the same gifts. It was during this time that Tombo discovered his love of sports and all physical activities. As the years passed, he transformed from chubby to lean and muscular. With all the activity and work around the farm, by the sixth grade, his body was slowly turning into the body of an athlete.

Devault looked very different in those days. There was a quarry, and there were housing communities that were built by the quarry management to house their employees. One of those communities was in Devault and the other a mile down the road in Cedar Hollow. There was also a neighborhood tavern known as Rocco's Tavern. And, of course, the s slaughterhouse. Both of those neighborhoods no longer existed once the quarry closed.

There is no physical evidence that these neighborhoods ever existed at all, except in the memories of the few people that are still alive that remember them, and maybe in this biography. But, trust me, they did exist because we had friends and relatives that lived in those homes. What still remains, however, is the s slaughterhouse (which later became Devault Foods) and the Tavern.

There was a baseball field in the community where the men of the community would get together to play. A generation later, Tombo, with his friends and relatives, played on that same field. Like the communities that disappeared, this ball field also disappeared and now, in its place, is a shopping center.

There was also a Grange Hall where meetings were held, and an annual show was put on by members of the community. It was a typical vaudeville-type show with singers and dancers, tap dancers, and comedy routines. And Tombo was always in those shows. The Grange Hall is still there!

Tombo graduated from elementary school and was now going to General Wayne Junior High School in Malvern, PA. It was there that he started to excel in sports and physical education. He played football and wrestled and succeeded not simply because he worked harder than others but because he was fearless of opponents.

It was there that he met Joanne Stainback in study hall. She was a beautiful but very shy girl. So, it came as a surprise that she was the one who approached him. There were school dances and boy-girl parties, and little by little, they got to know each other. They became inseparable throughout junior and senior high school.

CHAPTER TWO
HIGH SCHOOL

By the time Tombo was enrolling in Great Valley High School, the Vietnam War had begun. There was no way to avoid it. You could only postpone your military service for four years by going to college. It was a very dangerous time to be a young male teenager, with the war constantly lurking in your thoughts as you tried to live a normal life.

Tombo grew up in the 1960s, an era that sort of changed everything in America. The Civil Rights Movement was during this time; Martin Luther King was leading the movement, meeting with President John Kennedy and other politicians. John Kennedy was assassinated in 1963, and while his assassination remains somewhat of a mystery, it is no mystery that he was in favor of civil rights and many were not. Martin Luther King continued his work fighting for civil rights and gave one of the most famous speeches of all time on the mall in Washington DC in front of thousands that came to be known as the "I Have a Dream" speech. Martin Luther King was gaining power as more and more African Americans were drawn to his message. Martin Luther King was assassinated in 1968.

While both of their deaths are shrouded in mystery, there is no doubt that their fight for civil rights most likely cost both men their lives. However, the civil rights movement could not be stopped, not even with both of their deaths.

The 1960s also gave birth to new music that would change the music world forever. Musical groups emerged from England, like the Beatles and Rolling Stones. There was Elvis Presley with his gyrating hips, and of course, the birth of motown. It was music so revolutionary coming from the African American Community in Detroit, and everyone loved it! For the first time in America's history, it was music that brought the African American and White races together. Our parents hated our music, but we didn't care. It was the music that was instilling a rebellious nature in our generation. We were all being educated and started to think for ourselves and started to question decisions made by our parents and our government.

Many decided to have as much fun as possible since they really didn't know whether they would be alive or dead in the next few years. People started to rebel: they partied hard, got drunk often, took drugs, and had sex. They grew long hair, and wore strange clothing, and defied their parents, who were clueless and unsympathetic to the world they created for their children.

The younger generation had every reason to be angry. The Vietnam War was not being fought by our parents; it was being fought by our generation. The Vietnam War was also not being fought by politicians' sons. Protests broke out all over the country but to no avail. It was an ugly war, with a public that turned against the soldiers, who, despite not wanting to fight in a war they didn't create, they were forced to do so. Upon their return, they were criticized, ostracized, and humiliated... It was embarrassing and disgraceful to our generation that our soldiers were treated in this manner. When the war ended in 1975, over 58,000 American soldiers died in Vietnam. It created a wound between our generation and our parent's generation, one that perhaps never healed.

It was during this tumultuous time that young people were trying to live normal lives going to high school. They were known as the "baby boomer" generation because of the explosion of our population after World War II.

As a result, a new high school was built. It was named Great Valley High School and was only a year old when Tombo enrolled. The school was beautiful. Classrooms were often lined with many large windows, the gym was amazing, and the cafeteria was huge, which was also used for school dances with live bands. It sat on a very large and open field, so there were practice fields for all sports, a baseball field, a soccer field, and a football stadium that could accommodate thousands of fans. Inside it had a large concert hall with a stage, arts and crafts classrooms, and a wood-shop. In the middle of the school was a very special open court-yard garden with beautiful exotic cherry trees and park benches known as the Senior Court because only seniors were allowed to use it because of its limited intimate space.

Still lurking in the back of every male student's head was Viet-nam. The pressure of not knowing one's fate in this war made many young men develop an aggressive, combative nature with no way to express their feelings in the classroom. Tombo felt this pressure as well and found a way to express it on the football field and on the wrestling mat. It made him a better player, and it made others on the team better players. It was a place he could take out his frustrations on opponents. He was a fearless competitor on the football field and on the wrestling mat. He was chosen by his teammates as Captain of the wrestling team. He was the center of the football team. The one who snapped the ball and started every play. He played both offense and defense in high school, never leaving the game. And it was there on the foot-ball field and wrestling mat where he discovered the competitive and combative person he was that he would carry with him throughout his entire life.

During one match against a very good team, it was coming down to the last two matches to see what team the victor would be. Tom usually wrestled in the 180-pound weight class, but the coach knew it might come down to the final match in what is known as the unlimited or heavyweight class. There is no weight limit, so it would not be unusual to find someone weighing 250 pounds. And so it was at this one match. His opponent was twice his size. The wrestling coach, Mr. Baker, pulled Tombo aside and said, "You can't just win this match on points; you will have to pin this opponent for us to win this match". And so, he performed that rare feat of defying the odds with a much larger opponent. He pinned his opponent, and they won the match. The feeling of defying the odds and becoming victorious is one of those defining moments in a person's life. It is a feeling he wanted to experience again in his life.

Meanwhile, his girlfriend, Joanne Stainback, was doing the same thing as an athlete. She was excelling in all her sports as well. She was well-liked and respected by everyone, still a bit shy, but she was one of the most beautiful girls in school, yet it was something she never realized. That quality of humility made her even more appealing.

She couldn't understand how she was voted Homecoming Queen. But she was, and Tombo was her proud escort for that honor. While neither would believe it, every girl in high school had a crush on Tombo, and every boy had a crush on Joanne. They were always noticed and always lit up a room when they entered. They both had that rare gift of charisma, people so special that others are just drawn toward them without them ever realizing why. They never understood it, never would, but it was something they could not control. They were special and what made them special was that they never felt that they were.

Aside from his success in sports, Tombo had a love of music and particularly the music of the times. The 1960s, as mentioned before, was a revolutionary time in the music world. It defined the emotions of a whole generation. It wasn't enough for him to just enjoy the music; he wanted to create it as well. He learned to play the guitar and found some others who shared his love of music. It wasn't long before they were playing together in a band they called "The Flares." A four-piece band: rhythm guitar, bass guitar, brass, and drums. And they all sang.

They rehearsed until they were ready to play for school dances. They were good and soon had other invitations to perform for some local clubs and weddings. And while the whole idea of music was to bring people together to have fun, there were times when things didn't go as planned, and conflicts would arise. Some of this had to do with rowdy crowds that had too much to drink, some had to do with jealous boys whose girlfriends flirted a bit too much with the band on their breaks, and some had to do with the racial unrest that was happening all over the country. At any time, one or more of these things would be just enough to escalate into violence. On several occasions, the band ended up in fights for no better reason than they were all good-looking, talented white boys having a good time playing music. Something girls couldn't resist.

Tombo was the first to tell the other band members that he had had enough and would be leaving the band. It was becoming too dangerous to continue as they were. Eventually, the others came to the same conclusion, and that was the end of "The Flares."

It was time to finish high school and graduate. Tombo's father never went to college. His mother, Lucy, attended Immaculata College for two years but never graduated because she married and felt she needed to raise her family and care for her husband.

Much later, however, she encouraged Tombo to consider going to college. But he really didn't make up his mind until Mr. Como, the high school athletic director and football coach, not only encouraged him but insisted that he go to college.

For some reason, he took a special interest in Tombo and made it a point to tell him that if he didn't go to college, it would be the biggest mistake of his life. Tombo was not only surprised but confused by this. You see, earlier that year, Mr. Como, for no apparent reason, decided that Tombo should not play the last few football games of his senior year even though he was Captain and one of the best players on the team. It made absolutely no sense to Tombo or anyone else.

It is the author's opinion that Mr. Como recognized the athletic talent of Tombo and decided he didn't want to risk him getting hurt his senior year and ruining his college athletic career.

Tombo applied and was accepted at Bloomsburg State College, Villanova, and West Chester State College. Tombo and his parents decided he would go to West Chester State College (now West Chester University). It was nearby and affordable. Even though his family could have afforded an Ivy League education, it was just not how Italian Americans spent money in that era.

Parents of that generation all experienced the Great Depression, something that was so awful to experience as children that it affected them for the rest of their lives. No financial decisions were ever made quickly. It was a generation that saved their money instead of investing it in anything.

Most people of that generation lived in the same house for their entire lives. They sometimes bought new cars but would drive them until they could fix them no longer. They cared about how they looked and the clothes they wore but never spent more money than was necessary on clothes or shoes. Every man needed a suit for weddings and funerals, and special events. And it was often the only suit they owned and the suit they would be buried in. They might have a couple of different ties to go with that suit; a black tie for funerals and a red striped tie for more festive events. Men's suits were black, navy blue, or charcoal grey.

Living room furniture was purchased only once, and in many Italian American families, they were covered with some hideous plastic covering so that the actual fabric was never touched by human skin or human clothes. The everyday furniture was purchased once for its durability and longevity.

Their children who had other interests in music, dance, or sports were often given the opportunity to pursue their interests within reason. Parents would agree to pay for music or dance lessons with the strict stipulation that if that child didn't practice every day, they would no longer pay for lessons.

Sports like baseball or basketball required very little investment. A ball, glove, bats, a basketball hoop. So, there were some youth sports available. Other sports like wrestling and soccer were only available starting in Junior High School. In those days, the sports equipment, uniforms, and even shoes that were needed for that sport were provided by the school. There were also late buses that drove athletes home after practices (or at least fairly close to where they lived).

From these humble beginnings to acceptance at West Chester State College was considered a major accomplishment in Devault. At every dinner table in Devault, parents told their children that Tombo was going to college and how proud they all were of him for doing so. He was the first and became the example for many that came after him.

His plans were made, and he could enjoy the rest of his senior year and looked forward to going to the senior prom and graduation with Joanne.

Joanne came from a different type of family. Her father grew up in North Carolina in a very poor family. He used to pick cotton as a young man. It was always hard, back-breaking work with little financial reward. He decided after high school graduation to enlist in the United States Navy. It was there that he started to excel and discover that there was another world of opportunity once his military career ended. He eventually attended college and medical school and ended up the head surgeon at Bryn Mawr Hospital, one of the finest hospitals on the Main Line of Philadelphia. He realized what education did for him and how it changed his life and wanted his daughter to have the same opportunities that he had. It was always his hope that Joanne would want to attend college, and he encouraged her to do so. Joanne was accepted at Appalachian State College in Boone, NC. She decided to major in Health and Physical Education. Was her future in place after high school graduation, or was it?

Tombo and Joanne had been inseparable since Junior High School. They had never dated anyone else. But now, graduation would put them in different states for the next several years. Joanne decided that perhaps it was time for her and Tombo to break up, date other people, and find out if they were really meant to be together.

It made perfect and logical sense, but in truth, Tombo was heartbroken. It was hard for him to imagine his life without Joanne, and his new reality left him with a great deal of doubt and a lack of self-esteem. He knew that Joanne would have no trouble finding male companionship with her exceptional looks and wonderful personality. He, on the other hand, had not the faintest idea how to be single since he had never been. He had no idea how to approach women, what to say to them, how to ask them out, or if he would even be interested in dating.

He realized that this transition would be much harder for him than for Joanne, and he felt somewhat lost and perhaps even a bit betrayed. He asked himself what he had done wrong for her to make this decision to break up. Was it just a practical decision since they would be states apart, or was it something else? Joanne was the only romantic relationship he had ever had, so there were no references or past experiences to determine what had gone wrong or if it had gone wrong. He wondered what he could have done differently. Maybe he didn't spend enough time with her or tell her what she really meant to him? Maybe she never liked him as much as he liked her, but there was no one else that interested her in high school. Maybe she knew that if she broke up with him in high school, the other boys would be too loyal or afraid of Tombo to ask her out, and she would spend her high school years alone. All of these thoughts went through his head while his lack of self-esteem increased, and so did the number of sleepless nights.

He was grateful, however, that this happened at the end of their senior year, sparing them both the need to justify or explain to their friends.

While everyone realizes that high school graduation changes everything, no one wants to admit that at the time. Everyone promises to stay in touch, and they don't, everyone promises to remain lifelong friends, and they don't. And boys tell their girl-friends that they will always love them, and sometimes that is not true either. Life gets in the way, careers take over, people move out of the area, they end up all over the world and raising fami-lies, and it just becomes impossible to retain intimate contact with some people, even people you were very close to in high school. It is not anyone's fault; it is just what happens. Classmates go to work, some go to college, some get married, some take a year off to travel, and some go to Vietnam.

The Vietnam War remained controversial, and the media didn't help by reporting atrocities (that happen in every war), making our soldiers appear as insane, unfeeling killing machines. They were labeled as" Baby Killers". As a result, they were ignored, insulted, and spat upon when they returned to the States. And the worst part of this is that they were drafted to fight and had no way of refusing to go to Vietnam based on how the draft lottery was done.

Once a year, all 365 dates were put on a separate piece of paper, folded, and placed in a large container. The order in which the data was drawn became your lottery number which corresponded to your date of birth. If your date was one of the last 100 from the container, you would not be going to Vietnam; if your number was pulled out of the box, you most likely would be drafted. Your life became the luck of the draw.

No, it wasn't fair, but that is how it was done to provide soldiers to fight in a war that no one wanted to fight. It didn't seem to apply to politicians or affluent and influential business owners and their sons, who were either rejected, excused, or assigned duties that would not put them in harm's way. There was too much at stake for anyone to question the integrity of the military.

Of course, none of this had anything to do with anyone from Devault, PA. A small hamlet of a community with most Italian Americans just struggling for survival and the hope for a better life that they had not achieved in Italy and had not yet achieved in the U.S. But they were Americans now and would do what was necessary to help the country and protect their way of life.

Tombo was the oldest in the community and was the first to go to college. His college education would eliminate him from the drafting process until his education was completed. He had four years to better himself, imagine a life he hoped to lead, and beyond that, was unknown.

It is not difficult to imagine that if there are factors that are telling you that you may only have four years to live, you might try to incorporate all the things you wanted to experience in life into those four years.

CHAPTER THREE

COLLEGE YEARS

He enrolled in West Chester State and was assigned a room in one of the dorms with a roommate, Fred Ryder from Media. Fred was a tremendous baseball player. They got along famously, but several months later, Fred announced that he would be dropping out of school to marry since his girlfriend was pregnant. He didn't really want to drop out of school but didn't feel he had a choice.

During the year, Tombo made friends easily, and a few of them decided to rent an apartment together for the next semester: Ed Madikovic, Corky Corcoran and Bruce Heller.

They rented an apartment, brand new and beautiful, almost too good to be true. But it was a college town, and there were always people trying to capitalize on that, so it was not unusual to find a new apartment complex close to the campus to accommodate students. They were called Cambridge Apartments.

Four men shared that apartment, all with different backgrounds and intellectual interests, and different majors. How they got along and why they got along remains a mystery. But there was a certain chemistry between them.

They had parties and, because of their different backgrounds and interests, they brought diversity to these parties that made them all fun. Their parties became legendary, and everyone wanted to be invited.

Tombo was the only one of his roommates who was an athlete and a Physical Education major. He continued to excel at football as the starting center on the team. He played first under head coach Bonder, who died, and was replaced by Coach Mitten for the remainder of Tombo's football career in college.

West Chester State College (now West Chester University) attracted some of the best athletes in the state, particularly in the Philadelphia area. The college was often chosen because it was convenient and affordable. It was also practical because everyone who graduated received a teaching certificate qualifying them as teachers in their specific disciplines.

However, what was so interesting about the football team was that it was attracting some of the finest, most gifted players from high schools who were not fortunate enough to be awarded an athletic scholarship. However, the talent of these football players created winning seasons, championship seasons, and invitations to play in Bowl Games.

Tombo played on the team both in 1967 and 1968 when they were invited to play in the Tangerine Bowl. And while they lost both years to Morgan State and Tennessee Martin, respectively, it was something few athletes get to experience in a lifetime.

Meanwhile, the residents of Devault, PA, were all watching the bowl games on T.V., rooting for one of their own.

Everyone who chose West Chester State College realized that teaching is a noble profession. There is a certain pride shared among teachers, knowing it is their responsibility to educate the next generation.

Tombo drove a modest Ford to and from college. He visited his parents every other weekend of his college career and for holidays. What that means is while we have spoken about the legendary parties (and they were!), those parties did not happen every week, but at the most twice a month.

In Boone, North Carolina, Joanne Stainback was pursuing her career in Health and Physical Education also. She didn't get home often, but she did come home for the holidays and semester breaks. Joanne's mother made sure to invite Tombo over for dinner often when Joanne was home visiting. Joanne had no objection to this and secretly looked forward to spending time with Tombo. But, she never quite got over that shyness, which is why she never invited Tombo over personally.

Strange as it sounds, the amazingly beautiful, intelligent, kind Joanne, who had only friends and no enemies on earth, suffered from insecurity. Perhaps that is why it was her decision to break up during their college years. Perhaps that is why she didn't communicate with Tombo when she was at college. Yet, when she returned home, and they were together, it was as though she had never left.

Then she would go back to school, the insecurity would set in, and she would not communicate with Tombo. If it wasn't for Joanne's mother, Tombo and Joanne might have never seen each other again!

Joanne went back to school in North Carolina after these visits, and their college careers resumed. Tombo's roommates changed over the years as, one by one, they graduated. By senior year he was sharing the apartment with Bob (Hutch) Hutchison, Bobby Cavuto, and Bruce Heller. These gentlemen remain lifelong friends.

Finally, in June of 1969, the football stadium at West Chester State College was filled with parents of the graduating class. Tombo's mother and father attended the graduation exercises but decided not to invite other relatives to the ceremony or to have a graduation party back at the family residence.

This is not as unusual as you might imagine for Italian American families. They often downplay personal accomplishments and those of their children. Such behavior... speaking of your children with braggadocio, their accomplishments, and then the audacity to have a party to celebrate such would be considered an act of vulgarity.

After all, perhaps those invited don't have children that are gifted students, or worse, they may not have the financial resources to send their children to college even if they are intelligent and worthy.

So, while this graduation was a milestone for Tom and Lucy, they didn't want to hurt anyone's feelings who was not as blessed as they were. They kept this great accomplishment to themselves and celebrated privately with their son.

Upon graduation, the modest Ford was traded for a Corvette. It was in a class of its own known as muscle cars in that era. Sleek models and powerful engines were being produced by all the car manufacturers to appeal to young consumers. And while each manufacturer tried to compete with the Corvette, the Corvette remained king. It was the car that everyone dreamed about and wanted to own. Tombo was humble about owning that car and would often let others drive it. He enjoyed sharing what he had with others.

The year 1969 was also the year that the book "The Godfather" written by Mario Puzo, was published. It was a story about the Mafia. Every Italian American read that book and cherished every word of it. Its success led to a feature film. It continued its popularity at the box office and to this day remains a classic film.

And while we, as Italian Americans, were all law-abiding citizens, each of us secretly wanted to be Michael Corleone, making life and death decisions for the good of the family. Of course, the objective of the " Mafia" was not to continue a life of crime by selling drugs, prostitution, gambling, etc. It was only a means to convert those illegal funds into legitimate businesses providing jobs for immigrants that were not being treated fairly or given opportunities available previously to only the white Anglo-Saxon protestants.

But make no mistake, every Italian American still feels that they are not quite good enough. As a result, they feel they have to work harder, become successful, and help others that are not as fortunate. It is sort of in the DNA of Italian Americans.

The reason I mention the book, The Godfather, is, like I said, everyone wanted to be "The Godfather" in real life. But, in real life, it was much safer to do it legally by going into politics.

Tombo's uncle, Teddy Rubino, was very involved in local politics and very well connected to all the important people. He was sort of a completely legal Godfather looking out for the welfare of those in his community. While Tombo never became personally involved in politics himself, he was fascinated by the process and would always be involved in trying to help others get elected.

CHAPTER FOUR

LIFE AFTER COLLEGE

What are the chances that the middle school you attended would hire you as a teacher? Yet, that is exactly what happened. Tombo graduated from college and was hired as a Health and Physical Education instructor and coach at General Wayne Junior High School in 1970.

Now he could apply his knowledge and share it with others. He enjoyed the challenge and interacting with over 300 students a year, all of which he knew by name. He was well trained and qualified and had the advantage of mentoring under Earl Metzler, a seasoned teacher and coach.

Then suddenly, his uncle Dan Fillippo died of a heart attack. His uncle lived but one hundred yards from the house where Tombo grew up. It was his uncle that took over the dairy farm that adjoined the property. His uncle left a wife, Mary, and three children behind, Daniel, Jr., Ronald, and Lorraine. Also, a large herd of cows and a barn where they were milked daily.

Most college graduates have the advantage of easing into their professions or careers as the years pass. But that was not meant to be for Tombo. He moved back home, attended the funeral of his Uncle Dan, and then learned that his father was having some health issues and going through tests. All of these issues played a significant role in his life, and he would have to deal with them all.

In addition to teaching every day, Tombo was up before dawn, making sure everything was running smoothly at the meat packing plant, then off to teach. It was an impossible schedule to look after the family business, teach, and coach.

By his second year of teaching, his father was diagnosed with heart problems. He was going to have his heart valves replaced, a very new and risky procedure. Fortunately for his father, Tombo was again dating Joanne Stainback, who just happened to be the daughter of the chief of surgery at Bryn Mawr Hospital in Bryn Mawr, PA.

Dr. William C. Stainback was one of the finest surgeons in the country and, as such, knew all of the other great surgeons as well. Dr. Stainback recommended the finest surgeon he knew that could perform this delicate surgery, and it was scheduled to be performed at a hospital in Alabama.

Travel arrangements were made, but on the morning that his father was scheduled to leave, Tombo received a phone call from his Dad that his mother-in-law had just passed away. Tombo's grandmother was now gone, and he was instructed that he had the unfortunate task of informing his mother as his father boarded the plane for Alabama. Last thing his father said to Tombo before hanging up. "Take care of everyone."

His father knew the risks of his surgery, and it probably crossed his mind that something could go wrong with the operation. So his last words to Tombo would remain with him for the rest of his " life..." take care of everyone".

There was no need for Tombo or his mother to leave Devault at this moment. The preparation and surgery would take hours and hours. As a family, they decided to wait until the surgery was over and spend the time at home looking after the welfare of the business as plans were made for the funeral of his grandmother.

The surgery went well, and Tombo and Lucy went to Alabama after the operation. It would take time before he could be released from the hospital to recover sufficiently to return home. Tombo and Lucy, therefore, returned to P.A. in order to attend the funeral services at Alleva's Funeral Home in Paoli.

His father recovered and returned to his home in Devault after the funeral. Tombo knew things were never going to be the same after the surgery but was relieved and delighted that his father was alive. He knew that there was no one else to take care of the family business, and the stress of running that business was more than he was willing to allow his father to continue to run on his own.

Tombo knew that he would have to resign as a teacher and coach. He spent his third and final year at General Wayne. He really loved teaching and coaching and only lost one football game during his three years there.

There was another opportunity for only a coaching job at Malvern Prep in Malvern, PA. Tombo decided to accept this coaching job since it would free up the majority of his day to work at the family business. He coached there for two years, had winning seasons, and loved it.

At one practice session, he was conducting a drill for the lineman. The blocking sled is a common piece of equipment for football teams. It is a strange piece of equipment that is made of steel with some padding to represent an opponent to block. Tombo was conducting a drill on the sled one particular day, but his players were not doing it correctly. He decided to demonstrate how to hit the sled and drive it forward. As he hit the sled, he managed to break the sled, something that never happens. He stared at the sled for several moments wondering how to fix it, in disbelief. However, when he turned around, the players were just staring at him with their mouths open, realizing that what they had just witnessed was something they never thought they would experience. No one ever breaks a blocking sled; they are meant to withstand anything a human can do to it. But, on this particular day, Tombo broke the blocking sled! None of his players ever looked at him the same again or ever questioned what he asked them to do.

As much as he enjoyed coaching, his life was about to change as he was about to embark on an enormous responsibility.

The last few years of his life were tumultuous, and the only relief he seemed to feel was reconnecting on a regular basis with the love of his life, Joanne. Joanne graduated and found work teaching and coaching in North Carolina. They often spoke on the phone and saw each other occasionally when she had time to visit her family in Berwyn.

Tombo's life was in P.A., and Joanne's family and their lives were in P.A. At some point, Joanne decided it was time to return to her roots and build a life with Tombo and raise a family. When she returned, it was as though she had never left. She and Tombo picked up exactly where they left off after all those years apart. They were destined to be together; they were more than just in love...they were soul mates.

The wedding took place on July 7, 1973, at the Wayne United Methodist Church in Wayne, PA. They both came from large families, and preparations were made. More than 400 people attended the wedding and reception that was held at the Stainback residence in Wayne.

The Vietnam War ended in 1975. A national collective sigh of relief was felt by everyone in the country. It was time to return to life, family, careers, and business ventures. There was optimism felt after the war. It was a good time for them.

Tombo and Joanne bought a house on Monument Avenue in Malvern, PA. Joanne found a job teaching and coaching in the Downingtown School District. They were both athletes; they ran often. Joanne and Tombo decided to train for a marathon (26 miles). During this time, Tombo had to train, so they would often run to work (about 7 miles), then work all day and run back. Joanne ran even further as she planned for the marathon, sometimes running 20 miles on busy roads and after dark. Tombo often scolded her unmercifully for running after dark, but she did it anyway. She wanted to run that marathon, and no one was going to stop her.

The day finally came, and they ran in the marathon in Philadelphia. They both finished the 26 miles. They continued to run for the rest of their lives and often trained for half marathons and special races for special causes.

When Tombo took over the business, there were about 20 employees, but something was about to happen that would change the business forever. His father was taking it easy but was always around checking on things to keep active. Maybe too active, no one knows for sure, but he started to have health issues with his heart again. After some testing, they felt that the surgery would have to be redone. So, once again, Tombo's father went in for surgery in the state of Alabama and had the valves replaced again, and this time, the results seemed to be better.

Running a meat processing facility does not mean that you go to work in a suit and spend all day in an office doing paperwork and answering the phone. Tombo had to know everything about the business, about the machines, about the meat, about sanitation, about his employees. No, he spent very little time in an office; you were more likely to find him unloading trucks, fixing machines, or driving a truck making deliveries, especially on weekends when no one else was available.

While he was doing these tasks, his father would relax and hang out in the office and sometimes take calls. One day he returned a call from the Burger King Corporation. The person on the other end of the phone answered, "Thank you for calling Home of the Whopper!".

Later, when Tombo returned to his office, his father looked angry and disturbed. Tombo asked what was wrong. His father explained that he returned a call and believed that the person called him a Whopper. . His father didn't know the term Whopper, but he associated it with the word WOP, which, as we all know, is a derogatory term that was attached to Italian immigrants. His father hung up on the person! His father said, "The man called me a wop.!

Tombo started to laugh. "Whopper is the name of a sandwich, Dad."

Tombo returned the call and set up a meeting with the Burger King Corporation in Norristown, and his life was about to change forever. Mom and Pop restaurants, diners, and sandwich shops were being replaced by the fast food industry. McDonald's, Burger

King, Wendy's, Taco Bell and Roy Rodgers were all being built at the same time.

Burger King had over 100 restaurants in the U.S. and was expecting to build more. They needed a supplier who could produce the meat for their hamburgers. Tombo signed the contract and provided the meat for a few Burger Kings in the local area.

Burger King was impressed with the product and service and informed them to be ready for more orders. It required special equipment with more technology to produce exactly the product they wanted. It was a huge investment, but it made them the only meat processing facility capable of providing exactly what they needed. Devault Foods, Inc. was created.

The growth was imminent as more Burger Kings were opened and more meat was needed. The company grew from 20 employees to over 100 employees in just a few years.

It wasn't long before they were contacted by Wendy's, another major fast food chain. Before long, Devault Foods was supplying burgers to most of the Wendy's and Burger King's on the east coast, a few hundred clients, and thousands and thousands of pounds of meat!

The company grew at an astounding rate, became more specialized, and needed more equipment to keep up with demand. Refrigerated trucks were purchased, and drivers with a CDL (Commercial Drivers License) were hired. More than thirty-five 18-wheelers were traveling up and down the east coast delivering products.

Those few words were spoken by his father before his heart surgery, "take care of everyone" became his "mantra" and haunted Tombo day after day. He was now responsible for hundreds of clients who were counting on him, consumers that were expecting a wonderful product to eat, and over a hundred employees counting on him for work, and there seemed to be no relief for any sort of personal time, family life, or relaxation.

The family of his deceased Uncle Dan Di Fillippo was struggling. The oldest son, Dan, tried to adapt and went to West Chester State College; he dropped out after the first year and went into a similar meat processing business that he set up in the barn that was once used for milking cows. He wasn't competing with Tombo at the time but providing another type of meat processing service, mostly butchering deer of hunters and beef cows owned and raised by locals.

Tombo and his business were expanding at an incredible rate, and he needed more space that was now occupied by his cousin, Dan. Tombo offered to buy the barn where Dan Jr. was operating his business and purchased it. Tombo later received a flyer about a meat processing facility that was going up for auction in Harleysville, PA, and encouraged Dan to consider it rather than start another building from scratch.

The facility was perfect. Dan purchased it with the money he received from selling the barn and property to Tombo. Dan went on to create a wonderful, successful company, married and had children. One more person succeeded and was influenced by Tombo.

They were processing thousands of pounds of ground beef each week to provide products for Burger King and Wendy's and while that was more than enough to keep everyone busy, it was decided to add meatballs to their list of products. It was decided to turn the barn into a meatball processing plant.

But now they were in another world. The gourmet food world. You don't just throw some ground beef together with some breadcrumbs and expect them to taste good. It is not that simple. To anyone whose family came from Italy, making a good meatball was considered a rare and sacred art form. Recipes had been passed down for centuries for exactly the right taste, a mixture of spices, texture, and the ability to absorb the sauce. And if even a small mistake was made of those ingredients and quantities were not exactly perfect, the meatball would fail, and the person who made the meatballs would suffer a lifetime of shame and humiliation in the family.

Now, if you understand that mentality and apply it to the business world, it is very simple. Either you make the best meatball you can possibly make, or no one will buy them, and you will quickly go out of business. Unlike simply trying another meatball recipe on your family that might forgive you for the last awful batch of meatballs you made, in the business world, you don't get a second chance. You must get it right the first time, or you go out of business.

So, the research began, the building was remodeled, and special equipment was installed. The tedious process of refining the meatball recipe began.

Down the road was Nick's Tavern, where they made their own homemade meatballs, and their meatball sandwiches became legendary. The meatballs were a secret recipe made by Faye and Theresa DellaPenna. The recipe was willingly shared with Devault Foods for one reason; they were tired of making meatballs!

Both of those women prayed that the recipe could be duplicated by Devault Foods, saving them hours and hours of making the meatballs by hand. The years of kneading cold meat on their hands were taking their toll.

So, the process began, and a batch was prepared as the two women tested them. It took several attempts to get the recipe just right, but when the two women approved of the recipe, the meatballs were produced on a large scale. The product was called Mrs. Di Fillippo's Meatballs as a tribute to Tombo's mother, Lucy, who also had the final say on the recipe. The meatballs were a huge success. Two women danced with joy, knowing they wouldn't have to make meatballs anymore. After that, Faye and Theresa always spoke about Tombo with reverence as though he was a saint. It was quite annoying!

In a few short years, the company grew, the barn that was once used for milking cows was transformed into a meatball processing plant, and his cousin Dan Fillippo acquired a meat processing facility, thanks to Tombo, and was thriving in Harleysville. Tombo didn't have time to think about the other life he led as a teacher and coach. It had been a great time of his life, an easier time of his life, but it was becoming a distant memory. His life had another purpose.

Tom and Lucy Di Fillippo (Tombo's parents)

Tombo and Joanne's home

Tombo's professional photo

Tombo and Joanne at Joell's wedding

Tombo and Joanne in High School

Tombo and Joanne with Joelle and Thomas Jr.

Tombo and Joanne's wedding (July 7, 1973)

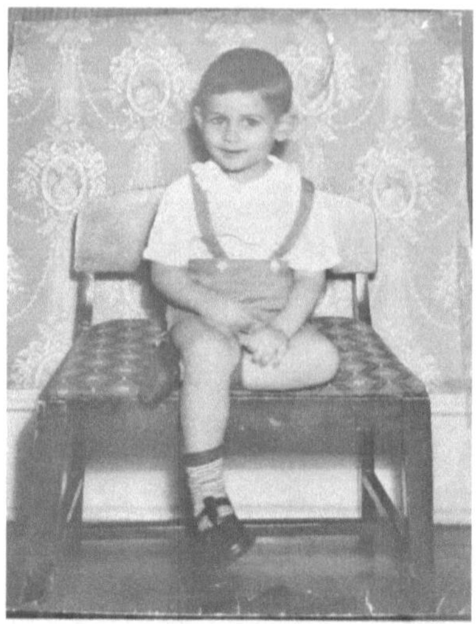

Tombo as a young boy

Tombo's grandfather, grandmother and their children.

Thomas and Tombo at Devault Foods Corporate Office

Thomas Di Fillippo, Sr. and grandson, Thomas

Wedding of Thomas and Erin Fillippo, from left to right (Tombo, Joanne, Thomas, Erin, Joelle)

CHAPTER FIVE

CHILDREN

Joelle was born in 1981. Joanne gave up her teaching career for her family. And while she missed her students, and they missed her, she was about to embark on that all-important life mission of raising children to the best of her ability.

Fortunately, Tombo was part of that mission but could not devote as much time because of his other responsibilities. Tombo, like many fathers, felt that twinge of guilt, knowing he would never spend enough time with his children. That balancing act between work and family plagued many men who became sole providers during that era. Men went to work, and women stayed home to raise the children. It is just the way it was for most people at that time.

Joelle was an amazing child that discovered a love of horses almost from the time she was born. Her parents encouraged her interest in horses as her love for those majestic creatures continued. Her love of horses continues to this day, often competing and returning home with ribbons and honors.

Thomas was born in 1984, and from the beginning, it was clear that he was a warrior. He was an amazing athlete, and somehow Tombo made time to attend practices or coach on teams that his son played on. His son was on a soccer team known as the Gila Monsters and Tombo always managed to attend practices despite his busy schedule. It was only a matter of time before the coach noticed Tombo, and they got to know each other. Soon the coach asked Tombo if he would like to help. Tombo knew very little about soccer, but what he did know about sports was that with all things being equal, the one deciding factor might be conditioning. Tombo and the coach talked about this, and it was determined that Tombo would become the conditioning coach of the Gila Monsters. At that point, the team was mediocre. Tombo instituted a conditioning program to put the players in better shape. Soon, the mediocre team was winning. Before long, the team was planning a trip to Europe to compete against teams in the Netherlands, Belgium, and France. Tombo and his son made two trips to Europe to compete in these events, something that most athletes never get to experience.

Thomas wondered how his father always found time to spend with him and his sister, Joelle. Tombo was always there for his son's sporting events and always there for his daughters' equestrian events. How he managed to do both and run the largest meat-producing facility on the east coast remains a mystery to his son.

Joelle and Thomas got the majority of their education in the Great Valley School District. However, when they moved from the house in Malvern, PA, to Valley Forge, PA, they attended the Conestoga School district.

It wasn't long before they bought the farm on Mine Road. It was a beautiful stone farmhouse of the previous century perched on a hill surrounded by 50 acres of both fields and forest.

Once they moved, Joelle and Thomas both went to General Wayne Junior High, just as their mother and father had. And like their mother and father, they both graduated from Great Valley High School and went to college.

Thomas went to Marshall University in Huntington, WV. He only spent a semester there before transferring to Elizabethtown for a year and a half. Then the 9/11 terrorist attack on the U.S. happened, and it sparked a fire within Thomas.

He made the decision to enlist in the Army and later became

an Army Ranger. He felt privileged that he led a good life and wanted to do something meaningful to protect that life.

His parents, in the meantime, were wrought with anguish, worried about him constantly, and wondered if he would return alive. It was a very difficult time for them. They were both distracted, often distraught, sometimes unable to concentrate on their own lives, and unable to convey their true feelings to others who did not have children in the war.

Their son wasn't just in the Army; he was an Army ranger, one of the best of the best. He was not just going to war to cook food or work on equipment; he was trained to do battle face to face with the enemy.

This reality was not taken well by his parents. Sleepless nights were common, and days trying to live a normal life were interrupted with constant anxiety. Festive events and holidays were shrouded with that nagging feeling of dread. Not knowing exactly where or what was happening with their son became a constant nightmare. It was impossible for them to live a normal life.

When his son told him that he wanted to serve, Tombo was immediately reminded of Vietnam and the trauma that he went through. And while Tombo wasn't called to serve, he had friends and classmates that did; some came home, some didn't. War is never pretty, and Tombo knew that. So, knowing that his son wanted to serve for all the right reasons didn't appease him. He knew that war would not only affect his son but might change his son and how he lived the rest of his life, and how all of this would affect him and Joanne.

It was the worst time of Tombo's life. Worrying about his son was more than he could bare or explain in words. He and Joanne didn't sleep, all they did was worry, but they knew that this was not their choice but that of their child. That was small consolation for them. Young people make decisions that their parents cannot change. And such was what was happening to them. For people that were usually in control of their lives, their professions, their employees, and their family, this was something beyond their control. And while they supported his patriotism and his devotion to this cause, it left them feeling hopeless.

Children will often do that to parents, but perhaps not on so grand a scale as telling their parents that they must enlist and fight. Thomas was one of those chosen individuals who felt compelled to do what was necessary to protect the American way of life. It is a rare calling, a warrior mentality, where individuals feel a certain obligation to do whatever is necessary and are willing to put their lives in harm's way.

The September 11 attack did that for many, and it was admirable. It was just that Tombo never expected that to happen with his own child. Now, he and his wife, Joanne, were powerless to protect him as they always had.

He told me that worrying about his son was the worst time of his life. Sleepless nights were common; trying to talk about it with Joanne was pointless... she was so upset.

Tombo reflected on the Vietnam War when so many of his friends and classmates were drafted since no one wanted to enlist. Vietnam was an ugly war, as they all are, but it didn't have anything to do with people invading our country as The September 11 attack did. So, it was difficult for Tombo and Joanne to justify their son's willingness to enlist.

But therein lies the beauty of people and what inspires them. They raised a child that was willing to fight because of 9/11. He was not alone, but he decided to do something others didn't do. He wasn't just going to enlist; he wanted to be part of the action, and he became an Army Ranger. He was going to do battle face to face with the enemy.

And while Tombo and Joanne were worried about him, I believe that deep down, they were afraid but amazingly proud that they had a son that was willing to do whatever was necessary to win. What bothered them was what bothers all parents; they want their children to be safe and to live normal lives. However, it is not the fate of many to do what is safe but to do what is right. It is not a fate to ignore what is happening and let others take responsibility. There are certain people that assume responsibility, feel compelled to serve, and do what is necessary. There is no greater patriotism than that. Thomas was one of those, who decided that he needed to do something to help, so he enlisted.

Yes, his mother and father didn't want that to happen for fear of his life. They wanted him safe, like all parents. They told him to really think about it before making up his mind. But his mind was already made up, and he wanted to enlist. His mother and father didn't try to stop him because they knew they couldn't. Then one night, a car arrived at their residence, and someone from the recruiting office knocked on their door. "Is Thomas ready to go?" Thomas said his goodbyes and climbed into the car. His parents watched him drive away, and the agony for them began.

He somehow managed to do three tours in Afghanistan and over 120 missions. When asked about the experience, he said he loved being an Army Ranger. And while this is a tribute to the soldier he was, his parents finally drew a breath of peace. What he put them through is something he may never realize, but since he returned safely was something they all could celebrate.

However, soldiers are inclined to do things that are not normal. It may bother them, or it may not. But being a soldier is a special calling; it requires a certain mindset, a certain understanding of the mission, and a certain understanding of the enemy. Sometimes soldiers are required to do things that will haunt them forever. It is the nature of war. What Thomas experienced in war may always remain a mystery. It is not uncommon for veterans to keep certain things to themselves. But it is often common and difficult for veterans to adapt to a non-violent type of life.

War did not just change Thomas; it also changed his parents. The constant anxiety experienced by families of soldiers is a gut-wrenching ordeal. As Tombo expressed to me during this interview with heartfelt emotion, I don't know how Joanne and I got through that. It was the worst time of our lives."

When Thomas finally returned after completing three tours of duty, it was perhaps the happiest day of his parents' lives. But they all knew that war had changed all their lives, and adjustments would have to be made by everyone. But mostly, Thomas would have to adapt to life in the U.S.

When he returned, he decided to finish his college education. He considered majoring in business but ended up majoring in History. He and his sister, Joelle, both graduated from West Chester University.

Thomas didn't have to worry about finding work. His father, Tombo, owned a thriving business, and his father needed help just as Tombo's father needed help at one time. It was an entirely different type of challenge, but Thomas was eager to learn, had a great mentor in his father, and was eager for the task and the challenge to succeed. Thomas did well, exceeded his father's expectations, and became a shrewd businessman in his own right.

Thomas eventually married Erin Zimmerman. They have four children; Thomas, Henry, Luca, and Winston, and they live not far from his father's farm.

Joanne and Tombo's daughter, Joelle, also lives close by and married David Kennedy. They had two children, Piper and Angus. Joelle's marriage with David ended in divorce. She eventually married Aaron Lynn and had a son, Landon.

CHAPTER SIX

BACK TO WORK

Now that Thomas was home, Tombo could concentrate more on his work. The business continued to expand. It was an exciting time, and the landscape was changing in America. Mom and Pop restaurants and diners were being replaced by the fast food industry at an alarming rate, and those customers needed a special product that few meat processing plants could produce without a sizeable investment and special equipment. Tombo had the foresight to invest in this equipment at just the right time and was prepared to produce as much as his customers needed.

They had almost three dozen 18 Wheelers delivering a product to Wendy's and Burger King restaurants on the east coast. It was even necessary to purchase a small plane for some deliveries.

Tombo learned to fly and did it often until one very hot summer day when he was coming in to land at the West Chester Municipal Airport. He knew he was not in the right position to land and felt he was going to run out of the runway and crash into the forest at the end of the runway. He made a split decision and pulled up on the nose, hoping to clear the tops of the trees and circle around for another landing attempt. Then disaster struck;

the landing gear was just low enough to catch the top of the trees. The wings were torn off, and the plane finally came to rest in a vertical position, with the nose of the plane touching the ground. As Tombo tried to free himself from the wreckage, he could feel airplane fuel leaking on him while sparks were flying.

He should have died on that day, but by some miracle, he didn't. Somehow, he managed to get to safety on his own, with barely a scratch. That was the end of the plane and his flying career, or more likely, once Joanne learned of this crash, she ended his flying career!

That near-death experience changed Tombo.

CHAPTER SEVEN

CHANGES IN TOMBO

If you had asked Tombo a year ago if he knew how to fish or sail, he probably would have answered something like this, "Fish? Sail? Are you crazy? People from Devault don't know how to fish or sail. It's farm country."

So, Tombo, what else don't people do in Devault?

"They don't ski. Do you know how much the skis cost? And all the other gear? And don't forget you have to go someplace where there are mountains, and there aren't any of those near Devault. So that means airfares and hotel expenses and meals. So, no, people from Devault don't ski."

Well, that was the old Tombo! The new, improved Tombo (who shouldn't be alive after the plane crash) is changing.

Joanne's parents had a house on the beach in North Carolina. Tombo, Joanne, and the children went a few times. Then they decided to buy a house next door to her parents, so they could go more often if they wished. So, yes, Tombo learned to fish and sail, and so did the rest of his family.

They also bought skis and gear and went on ski trips to the Rockies. Eventually, they purchased a house in Jackson Hole, Wyoming, where he spent many memorable vacations.

The plane crash may have been the best thing that could have happened to Tombo.

He was coaching his son's sports teams. Encouraging his daughter with her love of horses. Vacationing in the summer, skiing in the winter, and sometimes a motorcycle road trip with a few of his closest friends and cousins.

At some point in his life, early in his professional career, he decided to drop the Di from Di Fillippo. He became Thomas Anthony Fillippo. His importance and respect permeated the entire family. All of his cousins subsequently decided to do the same. They all dropped the Di and became just Fillippo's. It was time to buy the farm on Mine Road. It is about one mile from Tombo's work at Devault Foods. Joanne fell in love with that house, barn, and property at first sight. Tombo saw the look in her eyes, and he knew she should have the house of her dreams.

It is a farm of approximately 50 acres, with tall trees, two ponds, and a slight incline from the ponds to reveal a beautiful old stone farmhouse with a beautiful yard around it and a large stone barn. Not far is a small stone guest house. All of the buildings were made with Pennsylvania field stone found on the property.

Of course, when Tombo told his father that he was thinking of buying this farm, his father's first question was, "How much?" When Tombo told him, his father said it was too much and he shouldn't buy it. He should stay where he was and save his money. (Of course, Tombo's mother and father lived in a very modest house a few yards from the Devault Foods complex, and they lived through the depression, which changed how everyone from that generation thought.)

The old Tombo may have taken his Dad's advice because his father was a very astute businessman, but the new Tombo was going to be his own man, defied his father, and bought the farm he and his wife wanted!

It is here where Joanne and Tombo would spend the rest of their lives!

CHAPTER EIGHT
PHILANTHROPY

Looking back, it was a very hot summer day. Tombo was a small boy in the car with his father. They were driving to Norristown to pick up supplies. At an intersection, there was a policeman directing traffic. He was in the sun, his face covered with perspiration as he waved his arms, directing traffic. His father stopped at a store, bought an iced cold drink and walked it out to the policeman, and handed it to him. Tombo watched as the policeman seemed completely caught off guard by this random act of kindness. It was a lesson Tombo never forgot.

The difference between being generous and being a philanthropist is simple. Being generous is the act of doing something kind for someone, but they know who you are and can thank you. Being a philanthropist is about doing something kind for someone because it is the right thing to do, without expecting thanks or recognition. And it was in this realm that he found the most satisfaction.

He first became interested in philanthropy from an event raising money for leukemia. What he discovered was a group of like minds willing to help others less fortunate. Tombo thrived in this world.

He felt gifted, maybe even privileged to achieve the success he had achieved, and while it was his sole effort that made that happen, he was still grateful to be able to help others less fortunate, disabled, or suffering from some other personal crisis. . And what he loved about this work is that it made him happy to help others without them even knowing.

He was invited to functions for various charities and subsequently served on the board of directors of many of those charities.

But the joy he felt meeting and working with people who cared about the same issues energized him. He met each new challenge with alacrity. Those that worked with him welcomed his enthusiasm, his passion, and commitment to the cause.

Not all successful businessmen feel a need to help those less fortunate. Businessmen can be selfish, ruthless, arrogant individuals, spending their lives proving that they are better than others and feeling that they are entitled to live a life above and beyond other people. Taking time off from work for their own pleasure instead of helping others less fortunate. This was exactly the opposite of how Tombo viewed life.

He came from humble beginnings, and while he achieved more success than most, he never ever let that influence the person he was. He never joined a country club and could have, but he didn't have time.

As a result, many people who were deserving got that attention from him. And while most of those people didn't know he was behind certain decisions that would affect their lives, he was changing their lives for the better.

Scholarship awards, loans for business ventures, medical equipment for hospitals to save lives, and comfort stations for families to relax at hospitals became a priority in his life.

But there was another side of him, a more generous, without appearing to be generous, side. He learned that one of his cousins went into the roofing business. It was winter, a time when most roofing contractors had no work. Tombo hired him to do some work on the meat packing facility. When that roof was completed,

Tombo asked to have the roof replaced on a large garage. When that roof was completed, he wanted a new roof on the Devault Post Office Building across the street. That work enabled the new roofing company to make it through the winter and line up enough work for the rest of the year and years thereafter.

CHAPTER NINE

MEMBERSHIPS AND AWARDS

West Chester University
Chairman: West Chester University Council of Trustees
Board Member: West Chester University Foundation
Board Member: Sturzebecker Foundation

Community
Past Chairman: Paoli Hospital Foundation Board
President: Great Valley High School Alumni Association
Board Member: Central & Western Industrial Development Authority
Board Member: Chester County Industrial Development Authority
Board Member: Friends of East Whiteland Fire Company
Board Member: Mainline YMCA

Business
Past Chairman: Chester County Chamber of Commerce
Board Member: Chester County Development Council
Past President: Great Valley Regional Chamber of Commerce
Board Member DNB First Bank

Industry
Board Member: American Meat Institute

Past President: P.A. Meat Packers Association
Eastern Meat Packers Association

<u>Awards</u>
West Chester University Football Hall of Fame
Community Service Award: Chester County Boy Scouts
Business Leader of the Year: Great Valley Chamber of Commerce
West Chester University Distinguished Alumni Award
Order of the Purple Heart: Outstanding Citizen
Small Businessman of the Year: Chester County Chamber of
Commerce
TMACC: Citizen of the Year
American Meat Institute: Community Service Award
Great Valley High School "Wall of Fame"
Sturzebecker Hall of Fame
Chester County Business Hall of Fame

D evault Foods was doing well and had several hundred employees. No one who is that successful goes unnoticed by politicians, who need contributors and people who may be able to influence voters. Tombo never had a choice; it was inevitable that politicians were going to find him and ask for his help.

It started perhaps with his uncle Teddy Rubino, who was the county commissioner. Tombo and his other cousins were always involved in some way with Uncle Teddy's campaigns. And while Tombo had no interest in ever pursuing a political career himself, he became fascinated by the process and the strategies of politics.

He was particularly interested in local politics and how it affected the community, schools, and local businesses. At times he was asked to host fundraising events at his home on Mine

Road. At times they were intimate affairs with only a few important guests, and other times, rather large gatherings of a few hundred people.

The tennis courts would transform into a tented banquet hall, where fine wine and carefully prepared food were served before important speeches were made.

It was sometime before 2008 when Joanne and Tombo had Senator John McCain at their home for dinner. There has been a great deal written about John McCain and his remarkable life, spending years tortured as a prisoner of war in Vietnam and how he survived and became one of America's most beloved senators. He was standing next to Joanne in the kitchen when Joanne mentioned that her father was also a veteran. John McCain asked about her father and his branch. Joanne explained that her father, William Stainback, was Submarine Tender on the USS Proteus as part of the Pacific fleet. McCain almost choked on a piece of cheese. It turned out that John McCain and her father were on the same submarine tender and knew each other!

John McCain ran for President on the Republican ticket, losing the election to Barack Obama in 2008. They had different views politically but great respect for one another.

After the election, they became and remained friends until John's death in 2018.

In November of 1996, Tombo's father died. His death was felt by everyone in the community. And with that, Tombo had very little time to grieve, knowing that others were counting on him to run the business. And that is exactly what he did.

He buried his father and went back to work, which is exactly what his father would have wanted him to do.

There were other tragedies as well; he lost many in his family and eventually his mother. They all lived long lives, and while their deaths were felt by everyone, at least they lived long lives.

Joanne, the love of his life, was diagnosed with cancer. The nightmare began. The treatments and their lack of help. Tombo spent three years at Joanne's side during this period. Joanne died in 2018 and left her husband alone in the home they shared together.

No one lives a life without tragedy. But it doesn't make it any easier to know that. We live, and we love, and we hope, and then people we care most about are taken from us. And we are supposed to carry on without them. It is easier said than done. But that is what we do.

CHAPTER TEN

THE HOUSE

Sometimes the owner creates the house in which he lives, and sometimes the house has its own personality that cannot be changed. The original house was built in the 1700s; you walk into the room and feel its history. A walk-in fireplace where food was prepared and served, and a second floor for sleeping.

Other rooms were added over time. The house breathes and sighs. It creaks and moans. I had the pleasure of spending the night in that house and experiencing its personality.

The house is part of the land on which it was built. The stone from the ground and the wood from the trees on the property. The house is on a hill, and 50 acres surround it. There is a barn and a carriage house. There are two ponds that attract Canadian geese that have become annual residents. The fields that surround the house have a herd of deer. There are horses, donkeys, birds, and at least one fox. They all feel safe there, and Tombo enjoys their company.

But most of all, this is the house that Joanne loved. The furniture she selected, the artwork on the walls, the family photographs. It is not a house. It is a home. Her presence is felt in every room.

CHAPTER ELEVEN
REFLECTION

I asked a series of questions to summarize his life. Here are the questions and responses.

What makes you proud of your life?
I had enough time and was lucky to have friends to enjoy life with them.
What is the thing you cherish most about your life?
Children.
If you had one wish, what would it be?
That everyone lives in harmony.
If you were going to die tomorrow, what words of advice would you like to leave your children?
Be kind and thankful and love one another.
If you could change or recommend something that would make the world a better place, what would that be?
I would like the people of the world to respect one another.
If you had one year to live, how would you spend that year?
I wouldn't do anything different or special. I would spend that year exactly as I spent every other year.
What do you value most in life?

Family.

Is there a parting statement that you would like to leave your descendants?

Take care of each other and give back to people who have less.

ABOUT THE AUTHOR

Frank DellaPenna is a graduate of West Chester University, The French Carillon School, creator of the musical act Cast in Bronze, and author of several books.

As a musician, he performed for the Mass of Pope John Paul II, The NBC Today Show, Walt Disney World's Epcot, and numerous music and renaissance festivals across the U.S. for thirty years.

He now spends his time writing and composing music. He lives with his wife, Anne, in St. Peter's, Pennsylvania.

More importantly, however, Tombo and Frank DellaPenna have an interesting family relationship. Frank DellaPenna's grandfather, Rocco, came to America as a young boy of 16. His immigration was sponsored by Tombo's grandfather, Thomas Di Fillippo Sr., who agreed to house the young Rocco until he could support himself financially. Why would Thomas Di Fillippo Sr. do such a thing? It was discovered that Rocco'smother and Thomas Di Fillippo, Sr. were brother and sister.